THE WORLD OF
NASCAR

Tony Stewart

By Michael Teitelbaum

The
Child's
World®
www.childsworld.com

The
Child's
World
www.childsworld.com

Published in the United States of America by
The Child's World®
1980 Lookout Drive • Mankato, MN 56003-1705
800-599-READ • www.childsworld.com

ACKNOWLEDGMENTS

The Child's World®:
Mary Berendes, Publishing Director

Produced by Shoreline Publishing Group LLC
President / Editorial Director: James Buckley, Jr.
Designer: Tom Carling, carlingdesign.com
Assistant Editor: Jim Gigliotti

Photo Credits:
Cover: Joe Robbins (2)
Interior: AP/Wide World: 8, 11, 18, 20, 23,
25, 26, 28; Corbis: 6; Getty Images: 10, 12, 19;
Reuters: 15; Joe Robbins: 1, 2, 4, 16.

**LIBRARY OF CONGRESS
CATALOGING-IN-PUBLICATION DATA**

Teitelbaum, Michael.
  Tony Stewart / by Michael Teitelbaum.
    p. cm. — (The world of NASCAR)
  Includes bibliographical references and index.
  ISBN 978-1-60253-083-6 (library bound : alk.
paper)
  1. Stewart, Tony, 1971—Juvenile literature. 2.
Stock car drivers—United States—Biography—
Juvenile literature. I. Title.
  GV1032.S74344 2008
  796.72092—dc22
  [B]
                        2007049083

Contents

CHAPTER 1

4 **He's Just Warming Up**

CHAPTER 2

6 **A Fast Start**

CHAPTER 3

12 **Another Kind of Racing**

CHAPTER 4

16 **A Rookie to Remember**

CHAPTER 5

22 **Chasing History**

29 **TIME LINE**
29 **CAREER STATS**
30 **GLOSSARY**
31 **FIND OUT MORE**
32 **INDEX AND ABOUT THE AUTHOR**

[OPPOSITE]
*Tony Stewart has had the chance to shout
for joy after winning more than 30 races.
What's next for the two-time champ?*

He's Just Warming Up

LIKE CLOCKWORK, TONY STEWART HEATS UP WITH the weather every season. The NASCAR superstar is so good that he has a chance to win any race on the schedule. But when the days turn longer and the sun gets hotter, that's when he really puts it in gear.

Take the 2007 season, for example. Halfway through the NASCAR schedule, Tony stood in seventh place in the overall standings, but he hadn't won a race yet. Then, in the middle of July, in 80-degree weather in Chicago, Tony raced to victory. Two weeks later, it was even warmer in Indianapolis. Tony won there, too, in the Brickyard 400. "This time of year, it seems like we get hot!" he said.

Beginning with Chicago, Tony reeled off nine top-10 finishes in 10 weeks, including three wins. He earned a spot in the "Chase for the NASCAR Nextel Cup" (now called the Sprint Cup).

Tony's always near the top. In nine seasons entering 2008, he finished in the top 10 in the standings eight times. The one year that he didn't (2006), he was 11th. He figures to have lots of great racing seasons left. So while Tony already is one of the best drivers in NASCAR today, he just might be one of the best ever before he's through. In fact, think of it like it's the middle of summer for Tony's career—because he is just warming up.

[OPPOSITE]
Many years of experience gives Tony Stewart (20) the skills to battle nose-to-nose with anybody.

A Fast Start

TONY STEWART'S RISE AS ONE OF NASCAR'S superstars shouldn't really have surprised anyone. After all, he has had success racing lots of different vehicles ever since he was a child. As a youngster, he first showed the passion for racing that has driven him all his life. He also first showed his intense desire to compete, and to win. Sometimes that intensity has gotten him into trouble with other drivers—but more on that later!

Tony was born on May 20, 1971, in Rushville, Indiana. When he was eight, Tony's mother led him into the world of **go-karts**. Go-karts are small, motorized vehicles. They're very low to the ground and easy for young drivers to operate. Tony spent time after school and on weekends racing. When he raced, he often won.

At the age of 12 in 1983, Tony won the International Karting Foundation Grand National Championship. It would be the first of many victories in cars of all sizes, shapes, and speeds. In 1987, Tony captured the World Karting Association National Championship.

[OPPOSITE]
Like many drivers, Tony got his racing start on go-karts like these.

By the time Tony reached high school, he had moved up to midget cars. These are **open-wheel** cars that are miniature versions of big-time Indy cars. His excitement for racing and winning grew with each spin around the track. Soon, racing became the most important part of Tony's life. He made few friends in high school. Instead, he spent all his free time at the track.

Success came for Tony at the midget-car level, too. The United States Auto Club (USAC) organizes three

Tony's first high-speed races were in open-wheel midget cars like these. The steel bars protect the drivers in crashes and rollovers.

Driven to Win

One of the things that sets Tony apart from other drivers is his intensity. He has been described as "aggressive" and "fiery"—and a few things that aren't very nice! Whatever you call him, though, he has a single-minded focus on winning. Such intensity can lead to problems, though. He's lost his temper and gotten into arguments with other drivers or with **media** covering NASCAR.

Once, at a race in Loudon, New Hampshire, in his **rookie** season of 1999, Tony appeared to be on his way to victory. Then, with just two laps remaining, he had to pull in for a **pit stop**. He lost the lead and ended up finishing 10th. An angry Tony stormed from the track, refusing to talk to reporters. The press called the young driver **immature**. His reputation for being a "hothead" spread. "I am what I am," he told a reporter. "Take me or leave me."

Tony still is not afraid to show his emotions or tell other drivers or the media how he feels. "You know exactly where I stand," he says. But with each year, however, he has matured as a person and as a driver. He has also become one of the most generous athletes in sports. He's donated more than $1 million—three different times!—to the Victory Junction Gang Camp, a facility in North Carolina for kids who are sick. And in 2004, he was named NASCAR's Driver of the Year for his community support.

series of races on oval dirt tracks. Most young drivers begin with midget cars, as Tony did. They then move on to the larger Sprint series. The highest USAC level is in Silver Crown cars, which are the most powerful vehicles that USAC drivers race.

In 1989, Tony raced midgets on the USAC circuit. He won an award from racing fans as the best first-year driver. In 1991, he was voted the USAC Sprint Car Rookie of the Year. The following year, at the age of 21, Tony began racing full-time in the USAC in all three series.

Soon, Tony was competing in USAC races all over the Midwest. Sometimes he drove in three or four races,

These wild-looking machines are known as "World of Outlaw" sprint cars. The large wings on top help keep the cars from tipping over during turns.

The USAC was formed in 1956. Today, the USAC runs four major national series plus many smaller, local races.

in different states, all in the same weekend. In 1994, he was the national midget champion.

The 1995 season brought Tony the USAC's triple crown. He became the first driver to win championships in all three divisions in the same year. Only one driver, Pancho Carter, had won all three titles during a career. No other driver, however, had ever won all three in the same year. More people in the racing world began to take notice of this up-and-coming young driver.

3

Another Kind of Racing

ALMOST EVERY KID WHO GROWS UP IN INDIANA
and loves racing dreams of winning the famous
Indianapolis 500. He (or she) imagines racing down the
stretch and taking the checkered flag as the crowd roars!

Tony Stewart was one of those kids. But after going
as far as he could go in the worlds of go-karts, midgets,
and sprint cars, he had to choose what his next step
was. Would he follow his dream and move up to the
next level of open-wheeled cars, called "Indy cars"? Or
would he move over to stock cars and try to compete in
NASCAR, a lot like another Indiana youngster named Jeff
Gordon had done?

Tony decided on the Indy cars, and in 1996, he
joined the Indy Racing League (IRL). The IRL was a new
racing organization that grew out of the classic Indy 500
race. Because Tony was the sport's top young driver, his
success helped the group become well known.

In January of 1996, Tony finished second in a race
at Walt Disney World. It was the first race held by the IRL.
Then, in May of 1996, Tony fulfilled his dream by racing
in the Indianapolis 500 for the first time. He qualified for
the **pole position** with a speed of more than 233 miles
(375 km) per hour and even led the race for 44 laps. He
finished 24th and was the race's top rookie.

[OPPOSITE]
*Tony made the
move to open-wheel
"Indy" cars in 1996,
driving this high-tech
machine in the Indy
Racing League.*

13

A Winning Team

In 1997, Tony Stewart teamed up with Joe Gibbs, the man with whom he would achieve his greatest success.

Gibbs was the man in charge of Joe Gibbs Racing. He had been the head coach of the NFL's Washington Redskins from 1981 to 1992. Under Gibbs, the Redskins won three Super Bowl titles. Gibbs then took his coaching skills to the world of stock cars as an owner of a NASCAR team. Top driver Bobby Labonte already drove for Gibbs' NASCAR team. Gibbs, however, was always on the lookout for bright young talent. The young and talented Tony Stewart quickly caught his eye.

Tony has driven for Joe Gibbs Racing his entire career in NASCAR's top series. Gibbs returned to the Redskins as head coach from 2004 to 2007, but he still owned Joe Gibbs Racing. His son, J.D. Gibbs, ran the day-to-day operations for the NASCAR team while Joe was coaching.

The IRL staged only three events that year. That wasn't nearly enough to keep race-crazy Tony busy. So, although he had moved up a level, he still raced at all levels of USAC events. He also took his first step into the world of NASCAR racing.

NASCAR's top-level races are part of the Sprint Cup Series. One level below these are the competitions known as the Nationwide Series. When Tony first started out, there was a different sponsor, so it was called the Busch Series. Tony took part in nine Busch Series races in 1996. In these, he got his first taste of stock car racing.

In 1997, Tony finished fifth in the Indy 500, then went on to win the IRL series championship. That same year, he also competed in five Busch Series races. In 1998, Tony raced full time in the IRL. Still, he also drove in 22 Busch races.

Tony was gaining confidence and ability driving stock cars. He hadn't won a NASCAR race yet. But the scene was set. He soon would be a star on the biggest of all stock-car stages.

Tony was all smiles as he climbed into his now-familiar Home Depot car in 1999. The support of such major sponsors makes NASCAR possible.

4

A Rookie to Remember

BEFORE 1999, TONY HAD ONLY RACED IN THE
Busch Series part-time while still competing in the Indy
Racing League. But that year, he made the break from
Indy cars into stock cars full-time: Tony became a rookie
in NASCAR's top series.

The move from the Nationwide Series to the Sprint
Cup Series is a major one for any driver. For one thing,
Sprint cars are bigger and heavier than Nationwide
cars. That takes some getting used to, especially in the
heat of a race. Plus, the level of competition increases
dramatically. Sure, there are good drivers at every level,
but the Sprint Series represents the best of the best.
When Tony broke in, that meant his challengers included
drivers such as eventual four-time champion Jeff Gordon
and seven-time champion Dale Earnhardt Sr. Even Bobby
Labonte, Tony's teammate on the Joe Gibbs Racing team,
would prove a tough **rival**.

For those reasons, it takes most drivers years to win
their first Sprint Series race. It's rare for a rookie to win
even once. And yet, Tony won *three* times as a rookie in
1999. "None of us dreamed he'd win a rice in his first
year, much less win three!" team owner Joe Gibbs said.

Gibbs knew his young driver was good, but he didn't
realize he was that good. In 34 races as a rookie, Tony

[OPPOSITE]
After helping three
quarterbacks win
Super Bowl MVP
awards, Joe Gibbs
(left) hoped to make
Tony his MVD: Most
Valuable Driver.

Tony got off to a fast start. That's him on the left in the number-two starting position at the 1999 Daytona 500.

finished in the top 10 an amazing 21 times. He placed fifth or better 12 times. His three victories were the most ever by a rookie driver. And his fourth-place finish in the overall standings marked the first time in 30 years that a rookie had finished among the top five.

Tony's rookie year kicked off as the NASCAR season always does: at the Daytona 500. From his first **qualifying laps**, Tony showed the big boys that he meant business. Tony started the 1999 Daytona 500 in the number-two position. In the race itself, however, Tony finished 28th. With his first Sprint Cup performance under his belt, Tony was ready for more.

Doing Double Duty

Tony Stewart stopped driving full-time on the IRL circuit in 1999. But he couldn't resist getting back into an open-wheel car for the Indy 500 that year—even though he was entered in a NASCAR race the same day!

That's right. On May 30, 1999, Tony drove in both the Indy 500 and the Coca-Cola 600. He drove a remarkable total of 1,090 miles (1,754 km) in a single day.

The Indy 500 got underway shortly before noon. After more than three hours of racing, Tony finished ninth. The race ended at 3:15 P.M. He took a quick shower and was checked by the track doctor. The doctor cleared him to drive in the second race that night.

A golf cart brought him to a helicopter, which rushed him to a nearby airport. A private jet took Tony to the North Carolina, landing about 4:45 P.M. Another helicopter shuttled him to the Lowe's Motor **Speedway**. At 6:15 P.M., Tony took off in the Coca-Cola 600, starting from the 43rd, or last, position.

After 80 laps, he began to feel weak and tired. He pressed on, despite his continuing fatigue and **dehydration**. Tony finished in fourth place. His legs buckled as he climbed from his car. A medical team rushed to his aid. After some rest and lots of water, Tony was okay.

Tony was proud that he was the first man to drive in both races. He had completed more miles in one day than any other driver in racing history. However, he decided that NASCAR would be his future.

During Tony's next few races, he continued to improve steadily. He was gaining confidence in himself and earning respect from his fellow drivers. Tony's first victory came late in the season at a race in Richmond, Virginia. He dominated the race from the start, leading for 333 of its 400 laps. Perfect pit stops late in the race clinched the victory over Gibbs teammate Bobby Labonte. Tony became the first rookie to win a top series race in more than a decade.

"They're all special," Tony later said about his victories. "But when you win in this series, you beat the best."

Tony won back-to back races in Phoenix and Miami late in the year to bring his victory total to three. When Tony's remarkable rookie year ended, he not only was fourth among all drivers in points, but he also racked up 1,223 total laps, second only to Jeff Gordon. Tony earned more than twice as much money as any other rookie in NASCAR history.

It had been a great year, a record-setting one. Despite these achievements, however, the best was yet to come for Tony Stewart.

[OPPOSITE]
Tony wrapped up his record-setting rookie year by capturing the 2000 Pennzoil 400 at Homestead Raceway near Miami.

5

Chasing History

AS THINGS HAVE TURNED OUT, TONY STEWART'S
terrific debut season in 1999 was only a hint of things
to come. In the years since, he has clearly established
himself as a NASCAR superstar.

It may not have seemed that way in the early going
in the 2000 season. After his remarkable rookie year,
Tony expected to contend for the season championship.
But he got off to a slow start and was in 13th place in
points after nine races. Tony's hard work, though, kept
him moving forward. He also got some advice from
teammate Bobby Labonte, who would win the series
title in 2000.

"I know that I've got Bobby on my side," Tony
explained. "He's only a phone call away or he's right
there in the garage. Knowing that he's always close by
and has the experience is a big help."

Tony was also realistic. It was helpful to have a talented teammate. Once the race begins, however, each driver succeeds or fails by himself. "If it comes down to me and Bobby for the championship one year, then it's every man for himself," Tony pointed out. "However, I

Even with all his racing experience, Tony was smart enough to remember to learn from older teammates like Bobby Labonte (left).

Any Race, Any Track

Just like your favorite football team might play better indoors or on artificial turf, certain NASCAR drivers race better on certain types of tracks. Dale Earnhardt Jr., for instance, is at his best on the long, high-speed tracks such as Daytona and Talladega. Kurt Busch is best on the short tracks such as Bristol.

There's no way to categorize Tony Stewart, though. He is NASCAR's most **versatile** driver. The variety in Tony's racing background has helped make him a force on every kind of NASCAR track: superspeedways, intermediate tracks, short tracks, and road courses.

In 2006, for instance, Tony finished in 11th place in the overall standings. It was the lowest that he ever finished since joining the Sprint Series in 1999. But he also won five races—only Kasey Kahne, with six, won more. And Tony's wins came on three of the four different types of NASCAR tracks. He didn't win on a road course, but he did finish second on the road course at Watkins Glen. The next year, he won at the same track.

can't think of a better situation than to race Bobby for the championship. It would be great for our team. We could keep it in the family that way."

Tony soon posted back-to-back victories in Delaware and Michigan. He added another victory in a 300-mile (483-km) race in New Hampshire. It was only July, and Tony had already equaled his win total for the previous season. There was now little question that Tony was a rising star.

By season's end in 2000, Tony had won six times and stood in sixth place in the overall standings. Three more wins and a second-place finish followed in 2001. Surely a championship was just around the corner.

Tony and his teammates were full of optimism going into 2002. They couldn't wait for the season-opening Daytona 500. And then Tony finished in last place in the race. It was a disastrous beginning to the season. But

*Things don't always go perfectly for Tony. Here, he spins into the **infield** after hitting a wall.*

Tony didn't let the **setback** stop him. Three weeks later, he was back in Victory Lane in Georgia. By the end of the year, he edged Mark Martin to win his first NASCAR title.

"To rebound from finishing 43rd at Daytona, I still have a hard time believing we've done this," Stewart said in disbelief after wrapping up the championship on the last day of the season. "But there was no magic to it. It was just hard work."

Ever since that year, Tony's name is always mentioned among the championship contenders. He finished seventh in 2003 and sixth in 2004 before breaking through for his second title in 2005. He was without a win that season until the calendar said it was summer. Then, on June 26—the first race after the start of summer—Tony won in Sonoma, California. He went on to win five times in a seven-race stretch that carried him to the top of the standings. Tony thought his great run came thanks to some testing on the track during a race in Michigan, but maybe it was just his usual great run during the warm-weather months!

After Tony fell out of the playoff chase in the last race in 2006, he bounced back to finish sixth in 2007. For the ninth season in a row, he finished in the top 10 at least 10 times. He entered 2008 with 32 career victories in only nine seasons. He already ranked 19th (tied with Dale Jarrett) on NASCAR's all-time wins list.

[OPPOSITE]
Tony Stewart poses in New York City's Times Square with the 2005 Nextel Cup championship trophy.

There's no doubt that Tony is one of the top racers in NASCAR's Sprint Series. In fact, when it comes to driving ability, a lot of experts believe that only Jeff Gordon can rival the skills of "Tony the Tiger."

But where does that place him among the greatest drivers of all time? Well, consider that in the 60-year history of NASCAR, only seven drivers have won three or more season championships. Tony is one of another seven who have won two titles. The list of those 14 drivers includes all the great ones: Dale Earnhardt Sr., Richard Petty, Jeff Gordon, Darrell Waltrip, Cale Yarborough, David Pearson, Lee Petty, Ned Jarrett, and others. Tony is in some pretty incredible company there.

Mark Martin, the veteran driver who is well respected by NASCAR fans and racers, once called Tony

When you've had as much success doing what you love as Tony has had, it's hard not to smile!

"the greatest race-car driver in this era."

One day, Tony's long, fast road may take him to the very top . . . ever.

Tony Stewart

Time Line

1971 Born on May 20 in Indiana

1983 Wins the International Karting Foundation Grand National Championship

1989 Starts racing in the United States Auto Club series

1995 Wins the USAC triple crown, taking the midget, sprint, and Silver Crown class championships all in the same year

1996 Starts racing in the Indy Racing League and the NASCAR Busch Grand National Series

1999 Became the first NASCAR Cup Series rookie to win three races

2000 Doubles his victory total from the previous year, winning six times

2001 Finishes second in the Cup Series season standings

2002 Wins his first NASCAR championship

2005 Posts five race victories and wins his second NASCAR season title

Career Stats

YEAR	WINS	TOP 5	CHAMPIONSHIP FINISH
1999	3	12	4
2000	6	12	6
2001	3	15	2
2002	3	15	1
2003	2	12	7
2004	2	10	6
2005	5	17	1
2006	5	15	11
2007	3	11	6
Total	32	119	

Glossary

dehydration when there is not enough water in your body due to too much exercise or heat

go-karts smaller, gas-powered vehicles that are built very low to the ground

immature not behaving in an age-appropriate way

infield the area on the inside of the racetrack itself

media people who work for TV, radio, newspaper, or Internet companies that report news

open-wheel race cars without fenders

pit stop when racers leave the track and go to a special area called "pit road" where team members fuel the car and replace tires

pole position the best starting position—the inside of the front row

qualifying laps laps that are timed to determine who the 43 drivers for a NASCAR race will be, and in what order they will start the race

rival a person who competes against someone else

rookie an athlete in his or her first season in a sport

setback a defeat, or reversal of progress

speedway a paved track designed for high-speed auto racing

versatile able to do many things very well

Find Out More

BOOKS

Eyewitness NASCAR
By James Buckley Jr.
DK Eyewitness Books, 2005
A photo-filled look at all of NASCAR, including top drivers, history, cars, gear, and greatest races.

History of NASCAR
By Jim Francis
Crabtree Publishing, 2008
Find out where Tony fits among the other great champions and drivers from the first 50-plus years of NASCAR action.

Tony Stewart
By Tara Baukus Mello
Chelsea House Publishers, 2005
See how Tony compares to champions from NASCAR and other motor sports.

Tony Stewart: NASCAR Driver
By Wayne Anderson
Rosen Central, 2007
Another look at the two-time champion.

Tony Stewart: 2005 Nextel Cup Champion
By David Poole
Sports Publishing, Inc., 2005
Go back to the beginning of Tony's amazing career with this in-depth look at his road, from go-karts to NASCAR championships.

WEB SITES

Visit our Web site for lots of links about Tony Stewart and NASCAR:
www.childsworld.com/links

Note to Parents, Teachers, and Librarians: We routinely check our Web links to make sure they're safe, active sites—so encourage your readers to check them out!

Index

accidents, 25

Brickyard 400, 5
Busch, Kurt, 24
Busch Series, 14–15, 17

career statistics, 28, 29
Carter, Pancho, 11
charity activities, 9
Chase for the NASCAR
   Nextel Cup, 5, 27
childhood, 7
Coca-Cola 600, 19

Daytona 500, 18, 25
Driver of the Year, 9

Earnhardt, Dale, Jr., 24
Earnhardt, Dale, Sr., 17, 28

first NASCAR championship,
   27, 29

Gibbs, J. D., 14
Gibbs, Joe, 14, 16, 17
go-karts, 7
Gordon, Jeff, 13, 17, 28

Indianapolis 500, 13, 15, 19
Indy cars, 13, 19
Indy Racing League (IRL),
   13–14, 15, 17, 19, 29

International Karting
   Foundation, 7, 29

Jarrett, Dale, 27
Jarrett, Ned, 28
Joe Gibbs Racing, 14, 17

Kahne, Kasey, 24

Labonte, Bobby, 14, 17, 21,
   22–24
laps in one year, 21

Martin, Mark, 27, 28
media, 9
midget cars, 8–9, 10, 11

Nationwide Series, 14,
   15, 17
Nextel Cup, 27
nickname, 28

open-wheel cars, 8, 13,
   19

Pearson, David, 28
Pennzoil 400, 21
personality and temper,
   7, 9
Petty, Lee, 28
Petty, Richard, 28
pole position, 13

qualifying laps, 18

record breaking, 5, 19
rookie year, 17–21

speed, 13
sponsor, 15
sprint cars, 9–10, 11
Sprint Cup Series, 5, 9–10,
   14, 17, 24, 29
stock car racing, 14

teen years, 8–9
time line, 29
tracks, types, 24
training and hard work,
   7–11, 19, 27
triple crown, 11, 29

United States Auto Club
   (USAC), 8–11, 14, 29

Victory Junction Gang
   Camp, 9

Waltrip, Darrell, 28
World Karting Association,
   7

Yarborough, Cale, 28

ABOUT THE AUTHOR

Michael Teitelbaum has been a writer and editor of children's books and magazines for more than 20 years. He was editor of *Little League Magazine for Kids*, the author of a two-volume encyclopedia on the *Baseball Hall of Fame*, and the writer/project editor of *Breaking Barriers: In Sports, In Life*, a character-education program based on the life of Jackie Robinson.